I am pleased to endorse Lori's book. Lori's journey is, unfortunately, so common in the US presently. In the middle of her grieving, Lori threw herself into researching, learning and writing about her loss. On her journey, she wrote a powerful, short book about the shock of her loss and the effects of Adderall use on young people. The Washington Post reported on 3/14/23, "The rise in Adderall prescriptions was driven by adults 22 to 44 years old, for whom they increased 58 percent between 2018 and 2022, according to a Trilliant Health analysis of insurance claims nationwide. There were more adults receiving an Adderall prescription than those who had an ADHD diagnosis, the firm found." I encourage you to read Lori's story with hopes that tragedy is not repeated.

Myron E Ketter, LCSW, MAC
Licensed Clinical Social Worker
Master Addiction Counselor

Lori Perdue shares a heartfelt memoir of her daughter Meghan's life, from her delightful childhood, to her eventual struggles with addiction and ultimately, her death in childbirth. Her work reveals her own love and loss, and moves beyond the personal to discuss addiction and a health care system that failed Meghan and by extension her baby and her family. Lori's careful research into addiction adds depth and a framework to her narrative of a beloved daughter.

Jane E. Hearren, RN, CNM, MS

Lori has written her story to share a profound and painful life experience. With honesty and vulnerability, she writes about her daughter Meghan, of her birth and her life as she grew to be a young woman.

Lori has also written this story to share information about the medication Adderall. After extensive research on the uses and effects of Adderall, Lori tells how she feels that this drug contributed to changes in her daughter Meghan's personality.

As a mother, I admire Lori for being able to put her thoughts and feelings down on paper. As a nurse, I respect Lori's desire to educate readers on how a medication may have unintended effects on one's judgment, relationships, and well-being.

This is a cautionary tale but, more than anything, this is a story born of the deep love of a mother for her daughter and the desire to remember a very special person.

Jannie L. Hawkins, B.S.Ed., B.S.N., B.S.Nurs.Admin., R.N.

Archway Publishing books may be ordered through booksellers or by contacting:

Archway Publishing
1663 Liberty Drive
Bloomington, IN 47403
www.archwaypublishing.com
844-669-3957

ISBN: 978-1-6657-5287-9 (sc)
978-1-6657-5289-3 (hc)
978-1-6657-5288-6 (e)

Library of Congress Control Number: 2023921517

Print information available on the last page.

Archway Publishing rev. date: 11/13/2023

To my loving and patient husband, Tim,
who has been my rock through the real-life nightmare
of the past several years and my encouragement
behind writing this book.

It takes a great deal of courage to stand up to your enemies
but even more to stand up to your friends.

—J.K. Rowling

"She'll have to mourn some other way."
That is what my husband was told by my daughter's sister-in-law
when we rushed up to Virginia after hearing of her death.

I found out I was pregnant with Meghan after separating from her father while stationed overseas. It was quite an arduous marriage from the start.

I went back to the States to stay with my mother while I tried to figure out the next step. She knew I was struggling with what to do and thought I should have an abortion so I would not have to struggle raising two children on my own. I told her the baby was part of me and that I just could not do it.

I got a job at a temp agency doing secretarial work in downtown Pittsburgh and rented an apartment near my mother and sister. I worked up until the week or so before the delivery. It was a scheduled C-section, so I had a due date of June 5. Back then, if you had a previous C-section, then your other pregnancies would be delivered by C-section as well, regardless of the reasons. I'd had an emergency C-section with Meghan's brother two and a half years prior.

Somehow, I knew it was going to be a girl from the beginning. I even bought a cute pink-and-white jumper months before the ultrasound proved me right. When she was born and they laid her on top of my chest, I cried. She was the most beautiful baby. She was all fingers and toes. I remember thinking that they looked like spider legs, long and skinny. I never let her leave the maternity room I was in, and in those days, when you had a C-section, you were in the hospital for seven days. I thanked God for her.

Her father and I reconciled on the promise that things would change. When he returned to the States, we moved to Missouri. Back then, the town we moved to was nothing more than a truck stop off base. I was able to spend a lot of time with my baby girl. I studied photography at the community center on base, and I would take her with me on drives out in the country while I scouted sites. We would always take a plastic bag so we could pick up trash at the sites.

There were a few antique stores we would visit while her brother was in school. An older couple who owned one of the stores took a liking to her. They would look for Meghan every time I frequented the store, and they always had a treat for her. Everybody fell in love with this bubbly, blue-eyed toddler. We would go to the park where she would play with other toddlers. During the summers, I would take her and her brother to the lake. We made the best of a place that didn't offer much at the time.

I used to sing a song to her that she called the "Meghan song," which goes like this:

I love you, Meghan, oh yes I do

I love you, Meghan, because you're you

Oh, Meghan, I love you, oh yes I do

When she went to bed, I would say, "I love you from the top of the world to the bottom of the world and all over the world." Then she would say, "Mommy, sing the Meghan song." This was our nightly ritual.

She was so full of joy and such a happy child, always laughing, even at her own silly jokes. One day when she was about three years old, I was making spaghetti for dinner, and she came bouncing through the door and asked, "Mommy, is the basgetti ready yet? Get it? Basgetti ready?" Then she bounced right back out the door, laughing at her own little joke.

Another time, at the same age, she was left alone in the kitchen to finish her dinner. Suddenly, I heard her laughing. I walked into the kitchen, and she said, "Mommy, watch." She had a piece of food in her hand with our dog by her side. She raised the piece of food up over the dog's head and lowered it while chanting "Ears up, ears down." I had to hold my laughter back as I explained to her that she was teasing the dog.

When she turned four years old, she wanted her ears pierced because a friend of hers had pierced ears. I explained to her how it was done and that it was going to hurt, but she was persistent. We went to the local jeweler, and they sat her down, took the piercing gun, and did the first ear. She flinched, and I could see in her face that she was trying to be very brave. They did the second one, and a single tear rolled down her face. It tore at my heart. I picked her up, hugged her, and asked her if she was OK. She said, "Yes, Mommy." She never cried but that one tear. When she got home, she couldn't wait to show her dad and her friends her new earrings.

From Missouri, we moved to Indiana for two years, where she made her First Communion and started school. One of my favorite memories during that time is one trip she and I took to Pittsburgh to see my mother. She had gotten a little toddler's makeup kit with lipstick, and while we were driving, she proceeded to "make herself up." She put the lipstick all over and around her lips and her cheeks. There was a big truck coming up to her side, and she turned, smiled big with her smeared red lipstick smile, and waved at the truck. The driver must have had a good chuckle because he waved, gave her a big smile back, and honked. She was so proud of herself.

Then it was on to Virginia when Meghan was in the third grade. She was a good student and a social butterfly. She was in Girl Scouts (she started as a Daisy Scout in Missouri), and in the fifth grade she took up cello lessons. In high school she added crew team to her list of activities. She stayed with all three until she graduated high school, all the while maintaining good grades. She was a sweet, wonderful, wholesome teenager who never gave us any problems. When she was in about sixth grade, she went to visit her grandmother, and on a shopping trip with her, she made me a Build-A-Bear that would say "I love you, I love you" when you pushed the button in its paw. She said her grandmother told her I wouldn't want it. I still have that bear, and it's one of my favorite gifts from her.

Throughout the years, she and I would have what she would call "Mommy-Meghan" days where we would spend quality time together. Sometimes we just hung out together, some days we shopped and dined together, and other days we just saw a movie. When she was growing up, we saw just about every Disney movie that came out. I always looked forward to those times and will keep them forever in my heart. One of those Mommy-Meghan days turned into a weekend trip to Virginia Beach, where she introduced me to *Finding Nemo*. We had a lot of fun on that trip. We went dolphin watching, shopped, and, of course, sunbathed. She wanted to go parasailing, but I shot that one down. The mother and the nurse in me just could not give in to that one. One year, she made me a frame with a picture of the two of us in it. On the frame she wrote, "Mommy and Meghan." She also made a scrapbook one year for me, and in it she wrote, "Remember Mommy-Meghan days? I do." These are both treasured gifts.

Meghan was a worker bee. When she got a job, she was very dedicated to it, and she was thought highly of by all. I have mementos of all the places she worked at before going back to college in her late twenties. One very special memento is a Links of London charm bracelet that she gave me for my birthday one year. She added a charm to it on birthdays and Christmases over the years, each one representing special memories we shared together. I just recently added an *M* to it. Another is a beautiful antique Irish brooch she purchased when she was working in an Irish store. I have other unique gifts she brought me from some of her travels. I cherish these gifts.

One day, I walked into the kitchen as Meghan was making a cake for a friend's birthday. The cake was a Swedish nut cake that I made every holiday and for birthdays when requested. She loved that cake and told me that she wanted me to make it for the top of her wedding cake someday. I noticed as she was making the cake, she had her hands in the batter. I asked her what she was doing, and she stated, "I'm making the cake." I asked her why she was using her hands, and she said, "It says mix by hand." I explained to her that it meant with a spoon and not a mixer. She said, "But you use your hands when making meatloaf." She had me there!

Her senior year of high school, she became a fan of Frank Sinatra and reintroduced me to his music. I still listen to him and think of her. She and her friends rented (parents paying, of course) a 1950s-themed limo, and she dressed in a pink gown with a pink boa and white gloves up to her elbows. It was a happy time.

Her father and I divorced after she graduated high school. She and I remained close as we went to concerts together and met for dinner on several occasions. She was always introducing me to new music, such as Grace Potter and John Mayer, whose concerts we went to. She also introduced me to Ed Sheeran, whom I have a tough time listening to today without shedding a tear. She introduced me to new foods and new fashions. She loved to shop at Target, and we would meet up to shop there, then have dinner.

In 2011, I remarried. Meghan was excited for me and helped plan the wedding. She picked the date and helped pick the colors (which I later realized were her high school colors), flowers, and cake. It was so much fun. She even took one of my favorite pictures of that day. Tim and I were opening gifts with Meghan, his two children and nephew watching, and I fell asleep on Tim's shoulder. Mind you, we had a professional photographer but that picture remains my favorite.

Several months after our wedding, her father and brother moved to Kentucky. It was a government move for her father, and he enticed her to move with the promise of a government job. She spent six months or so with no job. She called me and told me she was depressed. She was afraid she would not get a government job. I told her not to wait for it and to look for other jobs. It was not long before she found work. She was successful, as always, and not only got a job but an apartment too. It was not long before she missed being with friends and decided to move to the DC metropolitan area. She was about twenty-eight when she started taking community college courses and was talking about being a counselor for veterans coming back from war. I was excited for her and told her she would be a great counselor. She was such a good listener.

After Tim and I married, we moved to Georgia for his job. Meghan and I remained close; she visited and called frequently. Around 2015, she started dating a young professional in the DC area. She said his sister was a psychiatrist and soon after told me she was diagnosed with ADD and had started taking medication for it. (According to The Child Mind Institute, ADD is an outdated term; the current term is ADHD and, in 1987, was revised in the DSM-3-R from ADD to ADHD). I was a retired registered nurse but not too familiar with adult ADHD. I did not question it because I never had any reason to not trust what she was saying, and she was an adult.

After a while, I started noticing personality changes, although they were subtle. She started to become argumentative. I found myself almost feeling like I was walking on eggshells when talking to her at times.

She also felt the need to diagnose her brother with Asperger's syndrome, though he has never been medically diagnosed. She and I both were trying to convince her father to get him help because he was without a job for several years and refused to actively pursue one. He would live a life of no responsibilities as long as he lived with his father. I could only guess she diagnosed him in an effort to find a reason why he was without a job and still living with his father. Her father and her grandmother let her believe that she would be responsible for her brother when her father died. I was so angry and told her father that it was a lot of stress to put on her. Instead of her father taking responsibility for her brother, he passed it on to her. I offered to pay half of the bills to get him help, but her father wouldn't budge.

Christmas of 2015, we had a little argument, and she didn't talk to me for a year. She invited us up to DC for Christmas, but I told her that her uncle and two cousins were coming to Savannah for Christmas. She invited us all and was adamant about it. For months, we planned the trip up until two weeks before Christmas, when she explained that her boyfriend's place was too small and that they found a VRBO for us to rent for $1000. The stress was becoming a little too much, so we declined and said we would come for another visit. She invited her father and grandmother up in our place,

and her boyfriend paid for the same VRBO for them. We sent Merry Christmas texts, then she just quit talking to me. It was bizarre behavior, unlike her. She ended up being convinced that she had to spend all her Christmases with her father and grandmother because her grandmother was getting older. She told me, "We don't know how much time we have left with her." Well, her grandmother outlived her. I felt her being torn and feeling like she had to take sides. I never talked about her dad or grandmother when Meghan visited us, but it was different when she visited her father and grandmother. If they had spent less time trying to passive aggressively get her to take sides and more time questioning her changes in personality, things might be different today.

I kept trying to call Meghan with no answer, and she never answered my texts. I was crushed. During that time, she broke up with her boyfriend and moved down to Fredericksburg to go to college there. Meanwhile, I had a friend whose husband was hospitalized, and I was going up there to help. I reached out to Meghan with fingers crossed that I might be able to see her while in Fredericksburg. The day after I texted, she answered back. I was elated! We talked like nothing had ever happened between us. I decided that it was all water under the bridge and never mentioned it again. I was so happy just having her back in my life. It was then that she told me she had decided to become a veterinarian and not a counselor. When I questioned it, she started to get upset, telling me that I was not being supportive. So I let it go. I was incredibly surprised by this change because math and science were not her strong points, and she had to take out a huge student loan to go to veterinary school.

She was working at a veterinarian's office and a small farm part-time while going to college. Then came calculus. She called me in tears because she could not pass calculus even with a tutor. I suggested she go to her education advisor to see where she could apply all the credits she had obtained. She called the next day to say that they could get her into a teaching program. She was upbeat about the idea.

While this was all happening, she told me she was having problems paying for her medication because she had no health insurance, so it was rent or medication. I offered to help by contributing a monthly allowance but explained to her that when Tim retired, I would not be able to continue as we would be on a fixed income. I told her that she might have to consider getting a job with insurance. She agreed. Little did I know at the time what I was contributing to.

I noticed more changes in her personality. She was becoming moody at times and reckless. She decided to visit a friend in California for spring break, and when I asked how she was paying for it, she told me she had extra money in her account. When she got back from her trip, she called me upset because she said the apartment manager's office lost the rent check. She was adamant she had dropped off the check before her trip. So we talked, and Tim and I advised her to go to the office to discuss it. After not getting anywhere with them, we helped her out by paying the rent. She then told me she discovered she spent the rent money thinking it was extra money in her account. I asked her if she was using a register to keep track of her money, and she said she wasn't.

Whatever amount she saw in her account she thought was extra money. So we discussed how to make sure she kept track of her money so she wouldn't forget her rent again. Also, what was concerning is while she was studying and working, she wanted to join an adult crew team, then she wanted help renting a cello so she could take lessons again. I could not keep up with all the things she wanted to do. When I questioned things, she got angry. This was not her normal behavior.

She eventually gave up on those ideas and started dating again. That kept her busy. She met a man and soon after brought him down to Georgia for us to meet. He had a degree in psychology and was working as a licensed practical nurse. While visiting, she started talking about politics, saying that we should never have gotten involved with the war in Afghanistan. She was getting a little out of hand with the discussion when her boyfriend gently nudged her and shook his head. I was surprised because years before, she wanted to help veterans who were fighting in that war. We kept busy that weekend and avoided certain topics of conversation.

It was not long into their relationship that she moved in with him. One night while in the apartment alone, she called to ask me if it was OK to take Xanax with Adderall. She told me a friend in the apartment complex gave it to her. I told her absolutely not and asked why she needed it. She told me she was feeling very anxious and needed something to calm her down. I told her if Adderall was making her anxious, she needed to call her psychiatrist to have her medication changed. She then told me she had already taken it. I asked when her boyfriend was coming home, and she said in the next hour. I told her to tell him she had taken it because, as a nurse, he could monitor her. I never did find out who gave her the Xanax or if she continued to use it with the Adderall.

They were getting serious in their relationship. It was early 2018 when she started talking about marriage and started sending me pictures of wedding dresses. I was excited for her and was thrilled to help her pick out the dress. That is every mother's dream. One day, she called me. In an irritated voice, she asked, "Are you going to pay for my dress?" I was thrown by her tone. I told her yes, that

I had not changed my mind. After visiting an Alpaca farm, she wanted Alpacas at her wedding. I was stunned. "Alpacas at your wedding?" I asked. Years before, all she wanted was a simple wedding. Her ideas grew exceptionally larger. I never did get to see her in her wedding dress.

Early November 2018, my mother passed away and Meghan, with her then boyfriend, joined my family and me for the memorial. They drove five hours up to Pittsburgh for the memorial, which was early evening. They ate, drank, and drove back later that evening. I asked them to spend the night, but they refused, stating that they would take turns driving. During her visit, she was quite talkative and animated and before she left, was making plans with her cousins to all meet down at our lake house the following summer. They and I were all excited and looking forward to it.

Two months later, she got angry with me and exploded. It was just after I had given her the last of her monthly allowances. This was when the troubles intensified. We tried to talk on the phone, but her anger just got worse. I asked, "Meghan, where is this anger coming from?" After that, she did not talk to me, and I thought if I just gave her time, she would come around. She never held grudges. After a few months, she announced her engagement on Facebook, which she had blocked me from, and my sister texted to tell me. I tried to call her to congratulate her, but she would not answer. Tim texted her fiancé to send our congratulations and ask why they did not tell us. Meghan texted Tim back, stating that I needed help and until I got it, she did not want me in her life. I had a breakdown. I felt as if I was in the twilight zone. Where was this coming from? I asked her what I needed help with, but she would not respond back. I knew then that she had started down a path she could not come back from. She dropped all communication with my family and her cousins. It was so surreal. To this day, I still cannot wrap my head around the intensity of her behavior. I know now it was the Adderall addiction, but the whole thing still seems all too unreal.

For three years, I tried relentlessly to reach her. My nephew said I put my ego aside to fight to get her back. Every time I tried to reach out, I got the same scripted response about how I needed to respect her boundaries and stop thinking about myself. And every time, I cried. I even tried to see her while I was visiting my good friend in Virginia in September of 2021, and she had her gate person tell me she was not home. I had family pictures for her that I thought she might like and left a note with them saying that I couldn't not try to reach out while in Virginia and that I love her.

The last time I reached out was late November 2021. I tried to apologize for whatever I did, which she still would not say, and again got the same scripted response. This time, she also said, "I am pregnant, and if you want to see your grandson, you need to get help." She added that it needs to be professional help, not a church counselor. By that time, I was seeing a psychiatrist due to my anxieties and the panic attacks I was having over all of this. I told her this and asked her what proof she needed, and she went silent. I cried till I could cry no more. I did get an "I love you" from her, and I took that even though it was followed by a "but." I still had hope, and I just kept telling myself that someday she would return. That Christmas, I sent a Merry Christmas message. That would be the last message I sent to my daughter. She died on June 26, 2022.

It was a beautiful day on June 29, 2022. It was my husband's birthday. When I got up that morning, he was outside on the porch talking to his son on the phone. I went out, kissed him on the head, and said happy birthday, then went in to start breakfast for him. A few minutes later, he came inside and in a somber tone, asked me to come outside so we could talk. I followed him and sat down, thinking he was going to tell me about his conversation with his son, and he did. What came out of his mouth next shook my world. He proceeded to tell me that his son has a college friend who was on Facebook with Meghan. This friend said that she died while giving birth to her son on the twenty-sixth. I tried to reach out to her husband, hoping it wasn't true, but he wouldn't respond. Still not wanting to believe it, I reached out to everyone I knew to prove she wasn't gone. I couldn't believe no one called to tell me. Not her husband, her father, or her brother. Again, was I in the twilight zone?

Later, a friend who is a nurse in the area told me it was true. I then found the GoFundMe page they set up to help with expenses. My stomach tightened so much as I cried that I thought I was going to die. My heart was torn apart, and I remember saying loudly, "No, no, no, no!"

My beautiful Meghan was gone. According to her death certificate, she died from disseminated intravascular coagulopathy (DIC), amniotic fluid embolism, and postpartum hemorrhage. No toxicology tests were performed. She was cremated soon after at her husband's request.

Four months later, her husband and her friends held a last-minute memorial with a few friends in attendance and others (if available) through zoom. She deserved so much more.

There is not enough research on Adderall abuse and maternal morbidity, but I cannot help but feel her long-term use was a contributing factor to her death. Taking Adderall is like taking speed for those who abuse it, and it wreaks havoc on your cardiovascular system over time. According to the Natural Institutes of Health (NIH) and PubMed Central (PMC), there is a small increased risk of preeclampsia and preterm birth among those who misuse ADHD medications. The risk of placental abruption increased in women who used the medication between weeks eight and eighteen of their pregnancy. I talked with a college friend who was a midwife for many years before becoming a nurse practitioner, working labor and delivery in a hospital for nearly twenty years. When discussing Meghan's cause of death, she proceeded to tell me how her patients who were on Adderall were monitored very closely during pregnancy. She also agreed with me that at Meghan's age and because of her Adderall use, she should have been considered high risk. My friend mentioned how her patients on Adderall were seen by a maternal-fetal medicine doctor. She also mentioned that a "hidden" placental abruption could lead to DIC and embryonic embolism. According to Cleveland Clinic, the difference between a revealed placental abruption and concealed, or hidden, placental abruption is that with a revealed placenta abruption patients "have moderate to severe vaginal bleeding" that is seen. With a concealed placental abruption, patients have "little or no visible vaginal bleeding. Blood is trapped between the placenta and uterine wall."[1]

As I write this, I wonder if her doctor knew she was on Adderall for so many years (then changed to Vyvanse)? If so, why didn't they look deeper into it? Did they know that her cardiovascular system was at risk due to her Adderall use?

A doctor should consider other methods of treatment before medicating their patients. Years ago, there was a push to consider diets for children with ADHD. There are claims that certain diets can help reduce symptoms of ADHD. According to an article in *Medical News Today*, "some research suggests the following specific diets- such as elimination diets, the Few foods diet and the Mediterranean diet – could play a role in managing ADHD."[2] Some studies suggest a gluten-free diet. Basically, what this means is that eating "clean food" and avoiding processed foods could help with symptoms. Recipes can be found online. It's actually quite simple: the foods you eat should be homemade and not packaged or processed. When Meghan was a baby, there were reports of glass being found in some jarred baby foods, so I bought a little grinder, and whatever I cooked for us, she ate as well. After hearing about a certain food coloring that was found to increase hyperactivity in children, she and her brother drank only real fruit juices. You learn by listening to and watching others; it was only

---

[1] "Placental Abruption," myclevelandclinic.org, Cleveland Clinic, May 3, 2023 my.clevelandclinic.org/health/diseases/9435-placental-abruption.

[2] Jayne Leonard, "What Are the Best Diets for ADHD?," medicalnewstoday.com, Healthline Media, last modified May 31, 2019, medicalnewstoday.com/articles/325352.

common sense to me at the time to give them real food. Not to say they didn't have the occasional happy meal but most of the time, it was home cooked meals. I spoke with one woman whose sixth-grade daughter has ADHD, and she, through research, has managed it by diet.

Other forms of managing ADHD in adults include cognitive behavioral therapies, relaxation techniques, meditation, and guided imagery are all helpful. Medication should be a last resort.

Also, it is very important to note the dangers of mixing Adderall and alcohol. Adderall is known to mask the effects of alcohol, leading you to drink more, which can lead to alcohol poisoning. It is also known that mixing the two can cause heart problems.

I have learned that adults do not "all of a sudden" have ADHD; it's something that starts in childhood. Children usually show signs in early childhood and are usually diagnosed before high school. According to the DSM-5, the symptoms usually start before age twelve. This is a change from the DSM-4 where the age of onset was seven years old. Meghan had no signs during childhood or early adulthood. According to Children and Adults with Attention Deficit/Hyperactivity Disorder (CHADD), adults with ADHD show problems with inconsistent performance in jobs or careers, losing or quitting jobs frequently, history of academic and/or career underachievement, relationship problems, and poor ability to manage daily responsibilities such as completing household chores, maintenance tasks, paying bills, or organizing things. Meghan did not show these signs until after she started using Adderall.[3]

After talking to a counselor who specialized in drug addictions, I learned that people who have ADHD take Adderall to calm down and help them focus. If a person who doesn't have ADHD takes it, it does the opposite. In a sense, it makes them act like a person who *has* ADHD and is not taking medication. Adderall is considered a study drug by some college students because it acts like speed and helps keep students awake and alert while studying. It's also called the "street-legal speed." I further found out that people on meth use Adderall when they can't get meth. Just like meth, Adderall is psychologically and physically addictive. Physical addiction is easier to recover from than psychological addiction, which gives a person feelings of grandiosity, invincibility, and intense well-being. According to the NIH, prescription stimulants like Adderall and Vyvanse increase dopamine and norepinephrine in the brain. Dopamine causes the brain to feel good. It is known as part of the body's reward system. So when increased by stimulants, it causes a person to have euphoric feelings and

---

[3] "Diagnosis in Adults," chadd.org, CHADD, chadd.org/for professionals/diagnosis-in-adults. April 1, 2023

helps them feel like they can take on anything. Norepinephrine increases alertness and attention. It also plays a part in the fight-or-flight response. It increases heart rate and blood pressure and affects the eyes (pupils dilate), heart, muscles, and other parts of the body. People taking Adderall without a diagnosis of ADHD also show signs of paranoia, which I was told she was experiencing. Meghan was never mean, never paranoid about anything and was actually pretty laid back until she started using Adderall. Another thing I learned is they will distance themselves from people who question their behavior and use of the drug. They tend to surround themselves with those who do not question their actions. Question anyway. The more people who question Adderall users' strange behavior, the more likely the users are to get help through intervention. They are drawn to enablers. When a person enables a drug or substance user, it is like making them a slave to their own insecurities.

I later found out that not only was she surrounding herself with people who would not question her but also others who were supposedly ADHD sufferers themselves. Is there an epidemic in millennials with ADHD, or an epidemic in the abuse of the drug? I also found out that there are numerous vlogs about adult ADHD that describe how you know if you have it. These people have no known medical background but can tell you how you might have it. I am astonished by this. People on social media should pay particular care when advising others on a diagnosis or playing up diagnoses for attention and likes. Instead, maybe they should tell people how to get treatment and that it doesn't always have to be with these medications. There seems to be a large following to these vlogs, which I suspect could be the cause of the increase in this drug being abused.

I also learned that her Adderall was changed to Vyvanse before she gave birth. They are both used to treat ADHD, and both carry cardiovascular risks. I am surprised that a doctor would prescribe her Adderall or Vyvanse without looking into her medical history. I wish I knew how she got that first prescription and, again, how a doctor could prescribe it without looking at her medical history and doing a thorough diagnostic interview to examine her for other psychological issues she may have been experiencing that would have led to a different form of help and possibly a different outcome. These medications should not be given just because a person states that they have problems focusing. These days with social media, it seems like a lot of people have problems focusing. They should be taught other ways to focus than given these dangerous medications.

When those addicted stop using the drug, they go through withdrawal for several days, even weeks. It's not pleasant and is a difficult thing to do. That is why a lot of people do not quit. Symptoms of withdrawal include fatigue, mood swings, heightened anxiety, disrupted sleep, increased hunger, gastrointestinal issues, irritability, lethargy, lack of motivation, panic attacks, uncontrollable crying, and depression, just to name a few.

Adderall is easy to get in colleges and easy to get through some doctors who do not explore a person's medical history first. I feel that needs to change. It is classified as a Schedule II drug, yet so readily available.

It is illegal to share medications for ADHD with another person and illegal to use them without a prescription. There are also legal ramifications for sharing any Schedule II drug.

I truly believe that if her father and her brother would've put their hatred of me aside instead of delighting in my daughter's sudden animosity toward me, they could've questioned her, talked to her, and helped her with her addiction.

Meghan always wanted to help people, and I write this to help others in her name. She had so much more to give and was taken too early in her life. I hope that her son will read this one day and know what a truly special person she was, especially to me.

Dear Meghan,

My Meggie Meghan, my sweet pea, my tickle toes, my loving girl, you will forever be in my heart, and I miss you so much.

I love you from the top of the world to the bottom of the world and all over the world.

XO
Mom

I'm not a psychiatrist, just a mom who has done my research and wants to share what I've learned.

This book is not written for any other reason than to educate and encourage, whether it be parents of children with ADHD or adults who have ADHD, to do their own research and find alternative ways to handle their diagnosis before using medications. I encourage any adult newly diagnosed to find a reliable psychiatrist who will do the appropriate testing and questioning before prescribing medication.

Remember, if you are not suffering from ADHD, taking medications like Adderall is like taking speed and when abused, can have deadly consequences.

Drug addiction comes in many forms. The most notable addictive drugs are meth and fentanyl, but don't discount prescription drugs like Adderall.

Acknowledgments

I want to thank all those who have helped in my research and contributed to this book through their knowledge, whether through their medical expertise or their own experiences with ADHD and the medications used.

Special thanks to Myron for sharing expert knowledge in drug abuse and leading me to the right areas of research, and to Jane, my friend from college, whose knowledge and expertise in pregnant patients who suffer from ADHD helped tremendously.

To those who have supported me through my grieving process, I can't thank you enough for being there. Mickie, David, Lisa, Angela, Jannie, Sherely, and Myron to name a few.

To Catherine, who planted the seed to write this book.

To Jannie and Jane, who took time to read and critique my book. You are all my angels.

I must admit, I was not the most graceful grieving mother, but how does a mother gracefully grieve?

Printed in the United States
by Baker & Taylor Publisher Services